# KISS ALEXA – Keep It so Simple

## Ambient AI, Alexa+, and the Caregivers Tree

By: Patrick J. Fischer

COPYRIGHT



First Edition: February 2026
ISBN: 979-8-218-68877-6 (Paperback)
ISBN: 979-8-218-71880-0 (E-book)
ISBN: 979-8-218-68879-0 (Audio)

Published by
Patrick J. Fischer
Accessibility Dot Net, Inc.

Printed in the United States

## Contents

# The KISS Principle Meets the Future

This book exists for one simple reason: to keep things simple. The KISS Principle has been defined many ways over the years, but in these pages, it means something very specific — Keep It So Simple. Not simplistic. Not watered down. Not dumbed down. Just simple enough that technology finally gets out of the way and lets people live their lives again.

That idea might sound obvious, but for the last twenty years we've been drifting in the opposite direction. Ever since the iPhone reshaped the world in 2007, technology has grown more powerful, more capable, and more efficient — yet also more demanding. Every year brought more apps, more notifications, more screens, more updates, and more steps between intention and action.

- We became faster, but we also became slower.
- We gained efficiency, but we accepted friction.
- We gained capability, but we tolerated complexity.
- Technology made us more productive — and at the same time taught us to put up with how long simple things now take.

I call this phenomenon Technology Airtime — the total amount of your life consumed by tapping, swiping, troubleshooting, charging, configuring, and staring at screens. And if we're honest, Technology Airtime has been rising for two decades straight. We've been living in a world where the price of using technology was thinking about technology all day long.

But something remarkable is happening now. For the first time in twenty years, Technology Airtime is going down.

Not because people are using their devices less — they aren't. Not because technology is slowing down — it's accelerating. The shift is happening because a new kind of intelligence has arrived, one that doesn't demand your attention, your eyes, or your hands. One that doesn't sit behind a screen or hide inside an app. One that doesn't require you to adapt to it, but instead adapts to you.

**This new intelligence is ambient AI.**

Ambient AI surrounds you without requiring you to look at it. It listens without intruding. It helps without interrupting. It fades into the background so your life can come back into focus. It is the opposite of the screen-centric world we've been navigating for two decades. It is the return of simplicity — the KISS Principle reborn for the AI era.

And the company bringing this shift to everyday life is Amazon.

Not because they were the first to talk about AI. Not because they had the flashiest demos. Not because they chased hype cycles. Amazon is leading because they built something that actually works — in real homes, for real people, every single day. Something that reduces Technology Airtime instead of increasing it. Something that restores independence, dignity, and ease — especially for people who have been left behind by traditional design.

**They built Alexa+.**

Alexa+ is not just a smarter assistant. It is the first consumer mainstream ambient AI voice assistant platform — a system that understands context, remembers preferences, adapts to routines, and responds conversationally without forcing you to think like a programmer. It is the first technology since the smartphone that genuinely changes the relationship between humans and machines.

And it does so by returning to the simplest idea of all:

Technology should serve people, not the other way around.

This book tells the story of how we arrived at this moment — how two decades of innovation, frustration, progress, and complexity set the stage for the rise of ambient intelligence. It explains why the old world of apps and screens reached its limits, and why voice-first computing is the natural next step. It explores how Alexa+ works, why it matters, and how it is reshaping independence for millions of people. It also shows you how to get Alexa+ today. If you already have an Amazon Prime account, then you already have Alexa+ and can begin using it immediately. To review Alexa+ pricing, see Appendix A.

In 2026, most adults are part of what I call the Caregiver's Tree. Every family has a family tree, but today there is something just as important: the network of people who support a loved one — children, grandchildren, cousins, neighbors, and friends — all connected by a shared desire to help.

Alexa+ becomes the trunk of that Caregiver's Tree. It provides the communication, coordination, and awareness that every modern family needs, and this book shows you exactly how to build that system in your own home.

**Ambient AI is the next evolution of that promise.**

Most importantly, this book shows that simplicity — real simplicity — is not a luxury. It is a necessity. It is the foundation of accessibility. It is the key to independence. It is the heart of human-centered design. And it is the future of AI.

You're about to dive into the blended story of three books — Ambient AI, Alexa+, and The Caregiver's Tree.

Together, they reveal a truth that has been hiding in plain sight:

When technology becomes simple, people become powerful.

And that is where our story begins.

## The Age of Attention Theft

Technology has always demanded something from us. Long before we had a name for it, long before we understood the cost, we were giving away pieces of our attention one tap at a time. At first, it felt harmless. A quick glance at a screen. A notification that needed a response. A message that couldn't wait. We believed this was the price of progress — the toll we paid to live in a connected world. But over time, the toll grew. The interruptions multiplied. The screens multiplied. And without noticing, we built our lives around devices that quietly consumed more of our time, our focus, and our presence than any generation before us.

We didn't call it "attention theft" back then. We called it convenience. We called it productivity. We called it staying connected. But the truth is that technology was slowly training us to serve it instead of the other way around. Every new device promised to save time, yet somehow, we had less of it. Every new app promised to simplify life, yet life felt more complicated. Every new feature promised to make things easier, yet our days became more fragmented. We were living in a world where technology demanded our constant participation — and we complied, because we didn't yet understand the cost.

Then came the era of Traditional AI. It arrived with great promise: smarter assistants, faster answers, more powerful tools. But Traditional AI lived inside the screen. It required us to go to it — to unlock a phone, open an app, type a question, navigate a menu. It was intelligent, yes, but it was also needy. It demanded our attention at every step. It amplified the very pattern we were already trapped in. Instead of freeing us from screens, it gave us more reasons to stare at them. Instead of reducing friction, it added new layers of interaction. Instead of giving us time back, it quietly increased what I would later call Technology Airtime.

Technology Airtime is the total time a human must spend interacting with technology to accomplish a task. It is the hidden cost behind every click, every swipe, every tap, every menu, every prompt. It is the measure of how much of your life technology consumes. And for decades, Technology Airtime only moved in one direction — up. We didn't see it because we weren't looking for it. We assumed technology was always making things faster, always making things easier. But the truth is that most technology was making things more complicated, more demanding, and more intrusive. We were losing hours, days, even weeks of our lives to unnecessary interaction, and we didn't even know it.

The world before Ambient AI was a world where technology required your full attention. You had to stop what you were doing, shift your focus, and enter the device's world. You had to adapt to its interface, its menus, its logic. You had to learn how to use it — and then relearn it every time it updated. Technology was not designed to fit into your life; your life was expected to fit around technology. This was the age of attention theft, and we were all living in it.

We built habits around interruption. We normalized distraction. We accepted that our phones would buzz, our apps would ping, our screens would light up, and our minds would fracture. We accepted that we would check our devices dozens, even hundreds of times a day. We accepted that we would lose minutes here and minutes there — never realizing that those minutes added up to hours, and those hours added up to days, and those days added up to a life increasingly mediated by screens. We accepted it because we didn't yet have an alternative. We didn't yet understand that technology could be designed differently.

Traditional AI was powerful, but it was also part of the problem. It required your attention — you had to go to it. It lived on screens — you had to look at it. It increased Technology Airtime — you had to interact with it. It was intelligence trapped inside a device, waiting for you to come and unlock it. And because we were conditioned to believe that more technology meant more progress, we didn't question the cost. We didn't ask whether technology should demand so much of us. We didn't ask whether intelligence could exist outside the screen. We didn't ask whether technology could serve us without consuming us.

This chapter is about that world — the world before Ambient AI. A world where technology consumed our attention instead of protecting it. A world where intelligence was locked behind glass. A world where every task required a device, every device required an interface, and every interface required time. It is the world we lived in for decades, the world we accepted as normal, the world that shaped our habits and expectations. But it is not the world we have to live in anymore.

Because something new has arrived. Something that doesn't demand your attention but respects it. Something that doesn't pull you into the device but supports you from the background. Something that doesn't increase Technology Airtime but dramatically reduces it. That something is Ambient AI — and it represents the first true shift in how humans interact with technology since the invention of the smartphone. To understand the revolution ahead, we must first understand the world we are leaving behind. This chapter is the doorway. The next chapters reveal the path forward.

## Traditional AI: Powerful, But Demanding

Traditional AI arrived with the promise of intelligence at our fingertips. It could answer questions, predict outcomes, recommend content, and automate tasks that once required human effort. It was impressive, even astonishing at times. But beneath the surface of its capabilities was a truth we didn't immediately see: Traditional AI was built on the same foundation as every other digital tool before it. It lived inside the screen. It required our attention. It demanded our presence. And because of that, it inherited the same flaw that defined the entire digital era — it increased Technology Airtime.

To use Traditional AI, you had to stop what you were doing and enter its world. You had to unlock a device, open an app, navigate a menu, type a question, or stare at a glowing rectangle. The intelligence was there, but it was trapped behind glass. It couldn't help you unless you went to it. It couldn't support you unless you shifted your focus away from your life and toward the device. It was powerful, yes, but it was also needy. It required your time, your attention, and your participation. And every time you interacted with it, you paid the cost in Technology Airtime.

We didn't question this at first. We were conditioned to believe that technology always required our attention. We were trained to think that interacting with a device was the natural way to access intelligence. We accepted the friction because we didn't know anything else. Traditional AI felt like progress because it could do more than the tools that came before it. But progress is not just about capability — it's about cost. And the cost of Traditional AI was hidden in the time it demanded from us.

Think about the steps required to use even the simplest AI feature. You want to know the weather? Unlock the phone. Swipe up. Find the app. Tap it. Wait for it to load. Read the screen. You want to send a message? Unlock. Tap. Type. Correct. Send. You want to control a device? Unlock. Navigate. Tap. Confirm. Every task required a sequence of interactions, and every interaction added to the total Technology Airtime of your day. Traditional AI didn't reduce those steps — it added new ones. It layered intelligence on top of complexity instead of removing it.

The irony is that Traditional AI was marketed as a time-saver. And in some ways, it was. It could answer questions faster than a search engine. It could automate tasks that once required manual effort. But the time it saved was often overshadowed by the time it demanded. The friction of accessing the intelligence often outweighed the benefit of the intelligence itself. We gained smarter tools, but we lost more of our attention. We gained convenience, but we lost presence. We gained capability, but we lost time.

This is the central limitation of screen-centric, app-centric, device-centric intelligence: it requires you to leave your life and enter the device. It interrupts your flow. It divides your attention. It forces you to adapt to its interface instead of adapting to you. Even the smartest AI becomes a burden when it requires constant interaction. Intelligence is not enough if the cost of accessing it is too high. And the cost, as I would later discover, could be measured — not in dollars, but in minutes, hours, and days of Technology Airtime.

Traditional AI was built for a world where screens were the center of gravity. It assumed that humans would always be willing to look down, tap, swipe, and navigate. It assumed that attention was an infinite resource. It assumed that the device was the natural home for intelligence. But these assumptions were wrong. Human attention is finite. Human presence is precious. And intelligence does not need to live inside a screen. Traditional AI was powerful, but it was built on a foundation that was already cracking.

This is where the contrast becomes clear — the contrast that defines this entire book:

"Traditional AI requires your attention — you go to it. Ambient AI requires almost none — it comes to you. Traditional AI lives on screens; ambient AI lives in your environment. One increases Technology Airtime; the other reduces it." This single distinction explains why Traditional AI, for all its brilliance, could never deliver on its full promise. It was trapped in a paradigm that demanded too much from the user and gave too little back.

Traditional AI was a step forward, but it was not the destination. It was a bridge — a necessary phase in the evolution of intelligence. It showed us what was possible, but it also revealed what was missing. It taught us that intelligence alone is not enough. For technology to truly serve humanity, it must respect our attention, not consume it. It must reduce Technology Airtime, not increase it. It must fit into our lives, not force our lives to fit around it.

The next chapter introduces the breakthrough that finally makes this possible — the shift from Traditional AI to Ambient AI. The shift from intelligence trapped in a device to intelligence woven into the environment. The shift from technology that demands your attention to technology that gives it back. The shift from a world where you go to AI to a world where AI comes to you.

This is the revolution. And it begins with understanding why the old way — the Traditional AI way — could never take us where we needed to go.

# Ambient AI: The Intelligence That Comes to You

For most of modern history, technology has required us to bend toward it. We learned its language. We memorized its steps. We adapted to its limitations. We accepted its interruptions. We shaped our lives around its demands. But what if technology didn't need us to come to it? What if intelligence could come to us — quietly, naturally, without friction, without screens, without stealing our attention? That question is the doorway to Ambient AI, the first form of intelligence designed to respect human presence instead of competing with it.

Ambient AI is not a smarter version of Traditional AI. It is a different species altogether. Traditional AI waits behind a screen; Ambient AI lives in the environment. Traditional AI requires your attention; Ambient AI protects it. Traditional AI increases Technology Airtime; Ambient AI reduces it. The difference is not incremental — it is foundational. It is the difference between technology that demands your time and technology that gives it back.

Ambient AI is hands-free. It is eyes-free. It is context-aware. It listens when needed and stays silent when not. It doesn't ask you to unlock a device, open an app, or navigate a menu. It doesn't require you to stop what you're doing. It doesn't pull you out of the moment. Instead, it meets you where you are. It adapts to your environment. It responds to your voice, your routines, your needs, your life. It is intelligence woven into the background — present, but not intrusive; powerful, but not demanding.

This shift is more than technological. It is human. For the first time, technology is learning to step aside. It is learning to serve without interrupting. It is learning to support without consuming. It is learning to fade into the background so that life can move into the foreground. Ambient AI is the first technology that understands that your attention is not a resource to be harvested — it is a resource to be protected.

For people who have been left behind by screen-centric design, this shift is transformative. The disabled community, seniors, and anyone overwhelmed by modern interfaces have long carried the burden of technology that was never designed for them. Screens assume sight. Menus assume dexterity. Apps assume comfort with complexity. Traditional AI amplified these barriers because it lived inside the very interfaces that excluded so many. Ambient AI removes those barriers. It restores independence by eliminating the need for screens altogether.

Imagine navigating your home without reaching for a phone. Imagine controlling your environment without touching a switch. Imagine getting information without staring at a screen. Imagine completing tasks without losing time. Ambient AI makes this possible. It turns the world itself into the interface. Your voice becomes the command. Your presence becomes the signal. Your environment becomes the canvas where intelligence operates quietly in the background.

This is why Ambient AI is not just a convenience — it is a revolution in accessibility. It levels the playing field by removing the very obstacles that once defined technology. It gives dignity back to everyday tasks. It empowers people who have spent years adapting to technology that never adapted to them. It transforms independence from a challenge into a default. And it does all of this by reducing Technology Airtime to near zero.

But the impact of Ambient AI extends far beyond accessibility. It changes how everyone lives. It gives parents more time with their children. It gives workers more focus. It gives seniors more confidence. It gives families more presence. It gives all of us more of the one thing technology has been quietly stealing for decades: our attention. Ambient AI is the first technology that understands that the goal is not to make us spend more time with devices — the goal is to help us spend more time living.

This chapter marks the turning point of the book because it introduces the intelligence that finally breaks the pattern of the past. Ambient AI is not about doing more with technology — it is about doing less with it. It is about reducing the steps, reducing the friction, reducing the interruptions, reducing the cognitive load. It is about lowering Technology Airtime so that life can rise to the surface again. It is about shifting from a world where we go to AI to a world where AI comes to us.

The next chapter explores the tension this shift creates — the tug-of-war between Ambient AI and everything that came before it. Because as Ambient AI rises, it challenges the assumptions, the business models, and the design philosophies that have shaped technology for decades. It forces us to confront a simple but profound truth: the future of AI will be defined not by how much it can do, but by how little it demands from us.

## The Tug of AI: Ambient AI vs. Everything Else

The rise of Ambient AI did not happen in a vacuum. It emerged in a world already shaped — and in many ways distorted — by decades of screen-centric technology. For years, the gravitational pull of the digital world moved in one direction: toward more screens, more apps, more notifications, more taps, more swipes, more Technology Airtime. The entire industry was built on the assumption that the future of intelligence would always live inside a device. But Ambient AI challenges that assumption at its core. It introduces a new gravitational force — one that pulls in the opposite direction. And between these two forces lies the great tension of our technological era: the tug of AI.

This tug is not subtle. It is not quiet. It is not theoretical. It is happening right now, in every home, every workplace, every pocket, every wrist, every pair of glasses, every app, every assistant. It is the struggle between two competing visions of how humans should interact with technology. One vision says: Come to me. Look at me. Tap me. Engage with me. The other says: Stay where you are. Keep doing what you're doing. I'll come to you. One vision increases Technology Airtime. The other reduces it. One vision consumes attention. The other protects it.

This is the tug of AI — the pull between Traditional AI and Ambient AI.

Traditional AI is the legacy of the screen era. It is powerful, but it is anchored to the device. It assumes that intelligence must be accessed through an interface. It assumes that humans must adapt to technology. It assumes that attention is available, abundant, and expendable. It is the AI that lives inside apps, inside menus, inside keyboards, inside screens. It is the AI that waits for you to come to it. And because of that, it is the AI that increases Technology Airtime.

Ambient AI is the counterforce. It is the intelligence that steps out of the device and into the environment. It assumes that technology should adapt to humans. It assumes that attention is precious. It assumes that the best interface is no interface at all. It is the AI that listens, observes, anticipates, and responds without demanding your focus. It is the AI that comes to you. And because of that, it is the AI that reduces Technology Airtime.

These two forces are not just different — they are opposites. They represent two incompatible philosophies of how technology should behave. And as Ambient AI rises, it exposes the limitations of the old paradigm. It reveals that the screen-centric world was never the final destination. It was a detour — a necessary but temporary phase in the evolution of intelligence.

But the tug is not just technological. It is cultural. It is economic. It is psychological. It is personal.

For decades, companies built their business models on capturing attention. The more time you spent on a device, the more valuable you became. The more you tapped, the more you swiped, the more you scrolled, the more profitable the system became. Traditional AI fit perfectly into this model because it required interaction. It required presence. It required attention. It kept you inside the device — and that was the point.

Ambient AI threatens that model. It reduces interaction. It reduces presence. It reduces attention. It gives time back instead of taking it away. It breaks the assumption that technology must always be in front of your face. It breaks the assumption that intelligence must always be accessed through a screen. It breaks the assumption that the value of technology is measured by how much time you spend using it.

This is why the tug of AI is not just a shift — it is a disruption. It challenges the incentives that shaped the last 20 years of digital life. It challenges the design philosophies that prioritized engagement over well-being. It challenges the belief that more technology always means more interaction. Ambient AI flips the equation. It says: The best technology is the one you barely notice.

But the tug is also personal. It plays out in the small moments of daily life. When you reach for your phone to check the weather, that is Traditional AI pulling you in. When you simply ask the room, "What's the weather?" and keep chopping vegetables, that is Ambient AI pulling you back. When you open an app to turn on a light, that is Traditional AI. When the light turns on because you walked into the room, that is Ambient AI. When you stare at a screen to read a recipe, that is Traditional AI. When the assistant reads it aloud while your hands stay busy, that is Ambient AI.

The tug is happening every day, in every task, in every interaction. And most people don't even realize it.

The tug is also emotional. Traditional AI often leaves people feeling overwhelmed, distracted, or dependent. It creates a sense of friction — a subtle but constant pressure to keep up, to check in, to respond, to engage.

Ambient AI creates the opposite feeling. It creates calm. It creates presence. It creates space. It creates the sense that technology is finally working with you instead of against you.

For the blind and low-vision community, the tug is even more profound. Traditional AI assumes sight. It assumes screens. It assumes visual interfaces. It assumes a world that many cannot access. Ambient AI removes those assumptions. It removes the barriers. It removes the friction. It removes the dependency on sight. It restores independence by eliminating the very obstacles that once defined technology. For millions of people, Ambient AI is not just a better experience — it is a lifeline.

The tug of AI is also generational. Younger generations grew up with screens as the default interface. They learned to navigate complexity. They learned to multitask. They learned to live with constant interruption. But even they are feeling the fatigue. Even they are craving presence. Even they are discovering that the most powerful technology is the one that demands the least. Ambient AI resonates across generations because it aligns with something universal: the desire to live fully in the moment.

As Ambient AI grows, the tug intensifies. Companies must choose which direction to pull. Designers must choose which philosophy to embrace. Users must choose which world they want to live in. The future of AI will not be determined by capability alone. It will be determined by which force wins the tug — the force that increases Technology Airtime or the force that reduces it.

This chapter is the hinge of the book because it reveals the conflict that defines the entire AI era. It shows that the battle is not between companies or devices or platforms. It is between two visions of how humans should interact with intelligence. One vision pulls us deeper into technology. The other pulls technology deeper into our lives. One vision consumes attention. The other protects it. One vision increases Technology Airtime. The other reduces it.

The next chapter reveals the metric that exposes the winner — the discovery of Technology Airtime, the gauge that explains everything, and the key that unlocks the true purpose of AI. Because once you measure the cost of interaction, the truth becomes undeniable: the future belongs to Ambient AI.

# Technology Airtime: The Discovery

Every breakthrough begins with a moment that seems small at the time. A detail overlooked. A pattern unnoticed. A question that lingers in the background until one day it refuses to stay quiet. For me, that moment happened in 1999 — long before the world talked about artificial intelligence, long before voice assistants, long before smart homes, and long before Ambient AI had a name. It began with something so ordinary that most people would never think twice about it: the difference between a mouse click and a keyboard shortcut.

The discovery of Technology Airtime didn't come from a lab, a research paper, or a Silicon Valley whiteboard. It came from a conversation I had in 1999 with an MIS director at a Fortune 500 company. This company employed several blind professionals who used Windows computers with screen readers. For those unfamiliar with how a blind person uses a computer: the keyboard is the primary input, and every piece of information on the screen is spoken back through synthesized speech. These employees worked in the same reservation system as their sighted coworkers.

Two weeks after the company upgraded that system, the MIS director reviewed performance reports and saw something astonishing: the blind employees were completing reservations 20% faster than their sighted peers. They were opening and closing reservations with a speed advantage no one expected.

The MIS director was stunned. He began observing how people actually used the new system. Within fifteen minutes, the reason became obvious. The programmers had redesigned the software to rely heavily on mouse clicks. Sighted employees were constantly shifting their hands — from keyboard to mouse, mouse to keyboard — while talking to customers. Blind employees, however, never touched a mouse. They stayed anchored to the keyboard, moving through the system with pure efficiency.

The company immediately went back to the programmers and removed every mouse-dependent command, converting the entire Windows-based system to full keyboard operation. And that moment — that realization that unnecessary interaction was the hidden bottleneck — is when the true definition of Technology Airtime was born.

Technology Airtime is the total time a human must spend interacting with technology to accomplish a task. It is the hidden cost behind every click, every tap, every swipe, every menu, every prompt, every screen. It is the measure of how much of your life technology demands from you. And once I saw it, I couldn't unsee it. I began noticing Technology Airtime everywhere — in workplaces, in homes, in schools, in daily routines. I saw how much time people were losing not to the task itself, but to the technology required to perform it.

For years, Technology Airtime remained a quiet truth — a private observation the world wasn't ready to hear. The industry was too busy celebrating new devices, new apps, new features, new screens. The assumption was always the same: more technology meant more progress.

But progress is not measured by how much technology we use. Progress is measured by how much time technology gives back.

And then something remarkable happened.

- AI didn't fail — it evolved.
- It began to step out of the screen.
- It began to move into the environment.
- It began to reduce Technology Airtime instead of increasing it.
- It began to become Ambient AI.

And leading that evolution — by a wide margin — is Amazon, with Alexa+.

While others were building AI that lived inside apps, Amazon built intelligence that lived in the home.

While others were building AI that required screens, Amazon built AI that required none.

While others were building AI that demanded attention, Amazon built AI that respected it.

Alexa+ spans every major part of daily life, anchored by the most common devices in each category:

- Home — Echo speakers, smart lights, smart plugs, thermostats

- Auto — Alexa-enabled cars, hands-free navigation, in-car media
- Health — medication reminders
- Wearables — Echo Frames
- Entertainment — Fire TV, multi-room music, personalized content
- Communication — calling, messaging, Drop In
- Productivity — reminders, lists, calendars
- Accessibility — hands-free control for blind, low-vision, mobility-limited, and aging users

Alexa+ has become the first true Ambient AI platform for consumers, and it has set the pace the entire industry must now follow.

This is the truth the world is waking up to:

Ambient AI is the next big thing — the next great leap forward.

Just as the smartphone transformed humanity by putting computing in our pockets, Ambient AI will transform humanity by removing the need to use computing at all.

Because the real obstacle to AI was never intelligence.

- The obstacle was interaction.
- The friction.
- The steps.

- The taps.
- The screens.
- The interruptions.
- The Technology Airtime.

Navigating life with AI is not about more AI — it is about less time spent using it.

It is about intelligence that comes to you instead of demanding that you come to it.

It is about Ambient AI.

Ambient AI is the first technology that aligns with the human experience instead of competing with it. It is the first technology that understands that your time is valuable. It is the first technology that gives back the minutes, the hours, the days that Traditional technology quietly consumed. It is the first technology that makes independence easier, not harder. It is the first technology that makes accessibility natural, not forced. It is the first technology that makes technology feel human.

This chapter marks the moment when the reader realizes that reducing Technology Airtime isn't just a metric — it's the Key 2 AI. It is the gauge that defines the obstacle. It is the lens that clarifies the future. It is the measure that determines which technologies will thrive and which will fade. It is the truth that explains why Ambient AI is not just better — it is inevitable.

Because once you measure Technology Airtime, the conclusion becomes undeniable:

- The future belongs to Ambient AI.
- The tug of AI — Ambient AI vs. everything else — is already underway.
- And the winner will be the intelligence that gives people their time back.

**This is the world we are entering.**

A world where technology finally steps aside.

A world where intelligence surrounds us quietly.

A world where presence returns.

A world where independence grows.

A world where Technology Airtime falls.

A world where AI comes to us instead of demanding that we come to it.

**This is the world of Ambient AI.**

And this is the world this book prepares you to navigate.

## Why This Book Exists

Technology was supposed to make life easier. That was the promise. Every commercial, every keynote, every product launch told us the next device would simplify our routines and give us more time. But for millions of people — especially those living with disabilities — the opposite happened. Instead of reducing friction, technology multiplied it. Instead of removing barriers, it introduced new ones. Instead of giving us time back, it consumed the time we already had.

Every new device brought a new interface to learn. Every update moved the buttons. Every app demanded its own account, its own settings, its own notifications. And every screen — whether on a phone, watch, thermostat, or refrigerator — demanded attention. Taps, swipes, scrolls, confirmations, permissions, updates. Technology became a full-time job.

For people with disabilities, this burden was even heavier.

- For someone who is blind or low vision, a screen is not a convenience — it is a barrier.
- For someone with limited mobility, a touchscreen is not intuitive — it is inaccessible.
- For someone aging into new limitations, constant UI changes are not improvements — they are disruptions.
- For someone overwhelmed by cognitive load, endless menus are not empowering — they are exhausting.

Technology, which was supposed to be a gateway to independence, too often became a gatekeeper. It required vision, dexterity, memory, patience — and constant adaptation to systems that rarely adapted back.

This book exists because that era is ending.

Alexa+ represents a turning point — not just in technology, but in philosophy. It is the first mainstream example of technology that adapts to people, not the other way around. It is designed to fade into the background instead of pulling you into its world. It treats accessibility not as an add-on, but as the foundation of the entire experience.

Alexa+ changes what independence looks like.

It changes what daily life feels like.

It changes what technology demands of us — and what it gives back.

For the first time, we have a system that reduces Technology Airtime — the hidden tax of modern life. Technology Airtime is the time you spend wrestling with devices instead of living your life. Alexa+ reverses that equation. It gives time back, especially to those who have historically paid the highest price in accessibility friction.

This book exists to show how Alexa+ restores independence in ways that were once unimaginable. It introduces the two breakthroughs that make this possible: ambient AI and large language models (LLMs). Ambient AI surrounds you quietly, helping without demanding your attention. LLMs allow Alexa+ to understand natural speech and respond with clarity. Together, they create a world where technology adapts to people instead of forcing people to adapt to technology.

This book exists to explain how ambient AI transforms daily life. It exists to show how voice-first computing levels the playing field for people left behind by screen-centric design. It exists to celebrate the dignity that comes from hands-free, eyes-free control of your environment. It exists to prepare readers for a future where AI fades into the background and life comes back into focus.

This is not a technical manual.

This is not a product guide.

This is a human story — the story of how technology finally learned to serve everyone. It is the story of a shift from complexity to simplicity, from screens to voice, from friction to flow, from dependence to independence. It is the story of how Alexa+ became more than a device. It became a partner in daily life — a quiet, ambient presence that restores time, dignity, and agency.

This book exists because the world is ready for technology that disappears so people can reappear.

It exists because accessibility is not a niche — it is the future.

It exists because independence is essential.

And it exists because Alexa+ offers the first real glimpse of a world where technology finally gets out of the way.

This is why this book exists.

# The Rise of Alexa

Amazon's journey into voice-first computing began quietly inside Lab126 between 2010 and 2013, where a small team worked under the internal codename Project D. Their goal wasn't to build another screen—it was to build a presence. A device that listened, responded, and blended into the background. That idea became the first Amazon Echo, released in late 2014 to a limited group of Prime members. It stood like a black cylinder on a countertop, always ready for a single word: Alexa. For many people, it was the first time technology felt ambient rather than demanding.

As Alexa's usefulness grew, Amazon shrank the hardware. In 2016, the Echo Dot arrived—a small, affordable puck that made voice access available in every room. Later that year, a second-generation Dot expanded that reach even further, turning Alexa from a novelty into a household network.

By 2017, Amazon pushed deeper into the smart home with the Echo Plus, the first Echo with a built-in Zigbee hub. It marked a shift: Alexa wasn't just answering questions anymore; it was orchestrating lights, locks, and sensors. The Echo family also softened its look with fabric covers and warmer design language, signaling that these devices were meant to live in the home, not stand out in it.

From 2018 to 2020, the lineup matured. The Echo Dot (3rd Gen) and Echo (3rd Gen) improved sound and design, while the Echo (4th Gen) introduced a spherical shape and integrated smart home hub. The orb design wasn't just aesthetic—it improved acoustics and made the device feel more like part of the room than a piece of tech. The Echo Dot (4th Gen) followed the same direction, and by 2022, the Echo Dot (5th Gen) refined the formula with better bass, faster processing, and environmental sensors.

Alongside the speakers, Amazon introduced the Echo Show line—Alexa devices with screens—beginning in 2017 and expanding through models like the Show 5, 8, 10, and the wall-mounted Show 15. These displays added visual context to the voice-first experience, becoming kitchen companions, communication hubs, and smart home dashboards.

Over time, Alexa moved beyond the home entirely. Devices like the Echo Flex, Echo Auto, Echo Buds, and Echo Frames explored new ways to bring ambient computing into daily life—plug-in assistants, in-car navigation, earbuds, and even smart glasses.

The history of Alexa devices is ultimately the story of a new interface. Amazon didn't just build speakers; it built a way of interacting with technology that didn't require hands, screens, or attention. Alexa introduced the idea that computing could be present without being intrusive—technology that waits quietly, listens respectfully, and supports independence in a way that feels natural.

## The Evolution of Alexa

When Alexa first arrived, most people saw it as a novelty — a clever speaker that could play music, answer trivia, and set a timer while your hands were full. But for many people with disabilities, Alexa was never a novelty. It was a breakthrough. It proved that voice could be more than a feature. It could be freedom.

Alexa wasn't perfect in the early days. It misunderstood things, had limited skills, and couldn't follow complex instructions. But even in that simple form, it represented something revolutionary: a computer you didn't have to see, touch, or navigate. A computer that came to you. A computer that listened.

For 35 years, I've worked with technologies that empower people who are blind, low vision, or visually impaired. To stay current, I've always been an early adopter — buying new devices the moment they came out so I could teach them and put them into the hands of the people who needed them most.

When Alexa launched, I bought one and installed it in my parents' home. My mom used it mostly for music. She loved classical pieces and simply said, "Alexa, play classical music." I even added a small Bluetooth speaker so she could carry the sound from room to room. No screens. No menus. Just her voice. She loved it.

For blind and low vision users, Alexa was the first device that didn't punish them for not having sight.

For people with mobility limitations, it was the first interface that didn't require reaching or swiping.

For seniors, it was the first modern technology that didn't make them feel behind.

For those who needed calmer environments, it was the first system that didn't overwhelm them with visual clutter.

Alexa's evolution didn't begin with engineering. It began with human need.

**The Early Years: Voice as a Tool**

In the beginning, Alexa handled simple tasks:

"Alexa, play jazz."

"Alexa, set a timer."

"Alexa, what's the weather?"

These weren't just commands — they were the first cracks in the wall of Technology Airtime. For the first time, people could interact with a computer the same way they interacted with another person.

## The Expansion: Skills, Smart Homes, and Routines

As Alexa grew, so did its ecosystem. Skills arrived, and suddenly Alexa could control lights, locks, thermostats, appliances, and entertainment systems. A person who couldn't reach a light switch could illuminate their home with a sentence. Someone who couldn't read a thermostat could adjust the temperature with a whisper.

Routines were especially transformative.

"Alexa, good morning" could trigger:

Lights turning on

Weather and news

Coffee brewing

Calendar events read aloud

This wasn't convenience.

This was independence.

The Maturity: Context and Conversation

Over time, Alexa became more conversational. It learned context, remembered preferences, and handled multi-step tasks. It understood natural phrasing instead of rigid commands.

People could say:

"Alexa, remind me to take my medication when I get home."

"Alexa, turn off the lights except the kitchen."

"Alexa, help me plan dinner."

Alexa was no longer a tool.

It was a partner.

The Turning Point: The Large Langaue Model - LLM (2023)

Everything changed when Amazon introduced the first version of Alexa powered by a large language model. In September 2023, Amazon publicly previewed a new Alexa built on an LLM — a Large Language Model optimized for natural, voice-first interaction.

For the first time, Alexa could understand language the way people actually speak it. It could reason, interpret nuance, and handle complex, layered requests that once required apps or screens.

For accessibility, this was monumental.

No memorized phrasing.

No simplified language.

No breaking tasks into tiny steps.

People could speak naturally — and Alexa understood.

But this was only the preview.

The real breakthrough was still ahead.

## 2025 - The Breakthrough Year: Arrival of Alexa+

February 2025 marked the moment everything changed.

This was the year Alexa+ became truly conversational — not just capable of understanding natural language, but able to reason, adapt, and respond like a partner who understood context, intent, and personal nuance.

This was the year Amazon launched Alexa+.

Alexa+ is not an upgrade.

It is a reinvention.

It represents the culmination of a decade of evolution — from voice assistant to ambient intelligence.

Alexa+ can:

- Understand complex, multi-step instructions
- Reason through ambiguous requests
- Adapt to personal speech patterns
- Learn routines without programming
- Integrate across devices and brands
- Operate hands-free and eyes-free
- Fade into the background

Alexa+ is the moment when technology becomes invisible — not because it's hidden, but because it's natural.

2025 was the year Alexa+ crossed the threshold.

The year conversation became the interface.

The year ambient intelligence became real.

**Why This Evolution Matters**

Alexa+'s evolution mirrors a larger shift away from screens and apps and toward presence, conversation, and ambient intelligence. It represents a future where technology supports life instead of interrupting it — where accessibility is the foundation, not an afterthought.

Alexa began as a voice assistant.

It became a smart home controller.

It grew into a conversational partner.

And now, with Alexa+, it has become something more:

a universal accessibility layer for the modern world.

This chapter isn't just about the evolution of a product.

It's about the evolution of an idea — the idea that technology should serve everyone, equally, without exception.

And that evolution is only beginning.

## Introducing Alexa+ and Ambient AI

For more than a decade, Alexa has been the voice that helped millions navigate their homes, their schedules, and their daily lives. But Alexa+ represents something fundamentally different. It isn't just a smarter assistant—it's the first version of Alexa designed to understand people the way people understand each other. With Alexa+, Amazon has shifted from voice commands to true conversation, from device control to genuine assistance, and from a collection of gadgets to an intelligent, adaptive ecosystem.

Alexa+ is built on a new generation of large language models that allow it to interpret nuance, context, and intent with far greater accuracy. You no longer have to remember the "right" phrasing or repeat yourself. You can speak naturally, change your mind mid-sentence, or ask for multi-step tasks in one breath. Alexa+ follows along, reasons through the request, and handles the details. It's the closest Alexa has ever come to feeling like a real partner in the room.

What makes Alexa+ transformative is not just its intelligence but its awareness. It remembers preferences, routines, and the devices you rely on. It adapts to your patterns without demanding your attention. It reduces the friction of everyday technology—the taps, the menus, the screens, the cognitive load—by meeting you where you are. For people with disabilities, seniors, busy parents, or anyone who simply wants technology to get out of the way, Alexa+ restores something rare: simplicity.

This new generation also expands Alexa's reach across devices. Whether it's an Echo speaker, an Echo Show display, a wearable, a Fire TV, or a third-party integration, Alexa+ brings a unified intelligence to the entire environment. It doesn't matter which device you speak to; the experience is consistent, conversational, and deeply personal. The assistant becomes the interface, not the hardware.

Alexa+ is more than an upgrade—it's Amazon's clearest expression yet of ambient computing. Technology that fades into the background. Technology that listens without intruding. Technology that supports independence, dignity, and ease. With Alexa+, the future of AI isn't louder or more complicated. It's quieter, more human, and finally aligned with the way people actually live.

# Upgrading to Alexa+

Alexa+ isn't just a new feature—it's a new brain. And the moment Amazon introduced it; millions of people naturally asked the same question: Can my existing Alexa devices be upgraded? The answer is yes for many devices, but not universally. Understanding what can be upgraded—and how to check—is the key to getting the most out of this new generation of ambient intelligence.

Alexa+ runs on a more advanced language model that requires faster processors, more memory, and a more modern audio pipeline than early Echo devices were built for. That means some older hardware simply can't support the new capabilities. But the good news is that Amazon designed Alexa+ to run on a wide range of existing Echo speakers, Echo Show displays, and Alexa-enabled devices released in recent years. For many households, upgrading is as simple as enabling the new experience in the Alexa app.

The best way to determine whether a device can be upgraded is to start with the Alexa app itself. Amazon built a compatibility check directly into the settings, allowing users to see which devices are eligible with a single glance. If a device supports Alexa+, the app will offer an upgrade path or a toggle to enable the new experience. If it doesn't, the app will clearly indicate that the device will continue running the classic Alexa experience. This approach removes guesswork and ensures that users don't have to memorize model numbers or release years.

Another reliable indicator is the device's generation. Most Echo and Echo Dot models from the last several years—including the spherical fourth-generation designs and the fifth-generation Dot—are fully compatible. Many Echo Show devices, especially the more recent 5, 8, 10, and 15 models, also support Alexa+. Wearables, Fire TV devices, and third-party products vary more widely, which is why the in-app compatibility check remains the most accurate method.

For users with older hardware, Amazon's approach is intentionally gentle. Devices that can't run Alexa+ aren't abandoned—they continue receiving updates, security patches, and the classic Alexa experience. But for anyone who wants the full conversational intelligence, adaptive routines, and multi-step reasoning that define Alexa+, upgrading to a compatible device is the most straightforward path.

In the end, upgrading to Alexa+ is less about replacing hardware and more about unlocking a new relationship with the devices you already own. The upgrade process is simple, the compatibility check is clear, and the benefits are immediate. Alexa+ brings a level of natural conversation and contextual understanding that transforms the entire ecosystem. For many users, the upgrade isn't just recommended—it's the moment Alexa+ finally becomes the assistant they always hoped it could be.

## How Alexa+ Connects Your Entire Home

Alexa+ represents a major shift in how people interact with technology, not because it demands new hardware, but because it frees you from thinking about hardware at all. Unlike traditional software that must be installed on each device, Alexa+ lives entirely in the cloud. The intelligence doesn't sit inside a speaker, a display, or a TV. It sits above them—accessible, consistent, and always improving. Any phone or tablet that can run the Alexa app, whether it's iOS, Android, or Fire OS, becomes a doorway into this new experience. The app is the universal gateway, the place where devices are discovered, upgraded, organized, and personalized.

This design means Alexa+ isn't limited by the device you're holding. You don't need a specific Echo model or a particular operating system. If your device can run the Alexa app, it can communicate with the Alexa ecosystem. That includes Echo speakers, Echo Show displays, Fire TV devices, and a growing number of third-party products. Each one connects to the same cloud intelligence, and each one benefits from the same improvements. The hardware doesn't need to run Alexa+ locally; it simply needs to connect to the service that powers it.

For consumers, this creates a rare kind of simplicity. You don't have to worry about compatibility charts or operating system versions. You don't have to think about whether your phone is "Alexa-ready." If you can install the app, you're in. And once you're in, every device in your home speaks the same language. Your Echo in the kitchen, your Fire TV in the living room, your Echo Show on the counter, and even third-party smart home devices all draw from the same intelligence. The experience feels unified because it is unified.

This cloud-first approach also means Alexa+ can evolve without requiring you to replace your hardware. When Amazon improves the intelligence, every compatible device benefits instantly. When new features roll out, they appear across your home at the same time. The intelligence grows, but your devices stay familiar. It's a model that respects the investment people have already made while still delivering the future of ambient computing.

Most importantly, this architecture supports independence. It removes the friction of learning new interfaces or navigating complex menus. You don't need to understand technology to use it. You just speak naturally, and Alexa+ handles the rest. Whether you're using a phone, a tablet, a speaker, or a display, the experience is consistent, predictable, and accessible.

Alexa+ isn't tied to any one device or operating system because it was never meant to be. It was designed to be everywhere you are—quietly present, always available, and ready to help. By living in the cloud and connecting through the Alexa app, it brings a single, unified intelligence to every corner of your home, no matter what devices you own or which platforms you prefer.

# The New Reality of Family Caregiving

The Caregiver's Tree is a term I created to describe a modern, connected way for families to support the people they love—especially when distance makes caregiving harder. Just as a family tree shows our roots and branches, the Caregiver's Tree shows how every branch of a family can stay linked through simple, everyday technology. At the center of this connection is Alexa+, acting like the trunk of the tree—steady, reliable, and always present—helping everyone stay informed, involved, and emotionally close no matter where they live.

With an Alexa+ device in a parent's or grandparent's home, families can share calendars, reminders, messages, calls, and updates across any distance. A daughter on the West Coast, a grandson overseas, a cousin in another state—each can contribute in small but meaningful ways. Alexa+ becomes the shared access point that keeps everyone aligned, turning caregiving into a coordinated, supportive mission rather than a burden carried by one person. The Caregiver's Tree ensures that even when families are spread across the country or around the world, they remain connected to the loved one at the center of it all.

## How Alexa+ Supports the Caregiver's Tree

The power of Alexa+ is not just in what it can do, but in how it brings people together. When you place an Echo or Echo Show in a parent's or grandparent's home, you're not just installing a device — you're creating a shared space where the entire family can participate in caregiving.

**Shared Calendars**

The Alexa app allows family members to add appointments, reminders, and events to a shared calendar. Doctor visits, medication times, grocery needs, therapy sessions — all can be added by anyone in the Caregiver's Tree. Alexa+ reads them aloud, reminds the person at home, and keeps everyone aligned.

Alexa+ supports all the major calendar platforms you're likely already using, including Google Calendar for full integration with your Google account, Apple iCloud Calendar for seamless sync with your Apple devices, and Microsoft Office 365 for work and business calendars. The setup process is straightforward across all platforms—simply navigate to your Alexa App, tap the More icon with three lines, select Settings, then Calendar, and choose Add Account. With shared email and calendar access, you'll discover the integration flows naturally, connecting effortlessly with your current workflow while offering voice control over your schedule both at home and in your vehicle's built-in system.

Beyond basic calendar access, Alexa+ delivers enhanced features that transform how you interact with your schedule. These include summarized calendar events, monthly and weekly views on screen-enabled devices, conflict awareness that alerts you to scheduling overlaps, and adjustable widget sizes on compatible Echo devices. The system also includes smart event detection—when you share files or emails, Alexa+ automatically searches for event details like names, dates, times, and locations. If it detects a single event, it adds it directly to your calendar and emails you a management link. For multiple events, it sends an email with suggested events for your review, making calendar management effortless and intelligent.

- A granddaughter can add a reminder for medication.
- A son can schedule a doctor's appointment.
- A neighbor can add a note about a home visit.
- Alexa+ keeps it all organized.
- Drop-In, Calling, and Messaging

Alexa+ makes communication effortless. Family members can call or message the Echo device without requiring the older adult to navigate a phone or screen. A simple, "Alexa, answer," is all they need.

Drop-In allows trusted family members to check in instantly — not to intrude, but to reassure. It's the digital equivalent of tapping gently on the door.

## Alexa Emergency Assist

Alexa Emergency Assist serves as Amazon's dedicated 24/7 safety and emergency response service, designed to provide households with rapid access to help during critical moments. With a simple voice command—"Alexa, call for help"—any Alexa+-enabled device instantly connects you to trained Urgent Response agents who can dispatch police, fire, or ambulance services to your location. The service operates hands-free across all Echo smart speakers and displays, plus the Alexa app, making it invaluable when speed and accessibility matter most.

The service incorporates intelligent safety monitoring that operates continuously in the background. Smart Alerts can detect sounds from smoke alarms, carbon monoxide detectors, security systems, and breaking glass, immediately sending notifications to your phone even when you're away from home. Subscribers can designate up to 25 emergency contacts who receive automatic notifications when help is requested, and the system stores critical medical information—including allergies, medications, and property access instructions—ensuring first responders have essential details without delay.

Alexa Emergency Assist costs $5.99 per month or $59 per year, positioning it as an affordable safety solution particularly valuable for older adults, individuals living alone, or families seeking enhanced peace of mind. The service replaces both the discontinued Alexa Together program and the previously free Alexa Guard features, consolidating emergency capabilities into a streamlined, subscription-based model. While separate from Alexa+, the services work synergistically: Alexa+ provides intelligent daily assistance and routines, while Emergency Assist delivers the reliable safety infrastructure every household needs. A limited free version offers basic features like designating a single emergency contact and 911 calling with certain carriers, though the full protective capabilities require the paid subscription.

**Daily Routines and Independence**

Alexa+ can guide a loved one through their day:

- "Alexa, what's my schedule?"
- "Alexa, remind me to take my morning medication."
- "Alexa, call my daughter."
- "Alexa, what time is my appointment?"

These small interactions add up to something profound: independence. The person being cared for doesn't have to wait for someone to call. They don't have to remember every detail. Alexa+ becomes their partner — gently, respectfully, and without judgment.

## A Connected Family, No Matter the Distance

The beauty of the Caregiver's Tree is that it doesn't matter where each branch lives. Some family members may be across town. Others across the country. Others across the world. But Alexa+ gives them all the same window into the life of the person they love.

**A Single Source of Truth**

Because Alexa+ lives in the cloud, every caregiver sees the same information. No more confusion about who added what, who changed what, or who forgot to update the group chat. The Alexa app becomes the shared notebook for the entire family.

**A Circle of Support**

Caregiving is rarely a one-person job. It's a circle. A team. A tree with many branches. Alexa+ strengthens that circle by giving everyone a role:

- One person manages appointments
- Another handles reminders
- Another checks in daily
- Another handles groceries or errands
- Another provides emotional support

Alexa+ doesn't replace the family — it coordinates the family.

**Preserving Dignity**

Most importantly, Alexa+ helps preserve the dignity of the person being cared for. They don't feel monitored. They don't feel dependent. They feel supported. Empowered. Connected.

They can ask for help when they need it.

They can communicate easily.

They can stay engaged with their family.

They can remain independent longer.

The Future of Family Care.

As families become more spread out and caregiving becomes more complex, tools like Alexa+ will become essential. Not because they replace human connection, but because they strengthen it. They make caregiving sustainable. They make communication effortless. They make independence possible.

## The Stewart Family and the Caregiver's Tree

When Mary Stewart turned eighty-four, her family realized something quietly but unmistakably: she was still sharp, still independent, still full of life — but she needed a little more support than she used to. Nothing dramatic. Just the small things that add up. Remembering appointments. Keeping track of medications. Staying connected with her children and grandchildren who lived across the country.

- Mary lived in Kansas City.
- Her daughter Elena lived in Denver.
- Her son Daniel lived in Miami.
- Her grandson Carl was stationed overseas with the Air Force.
- Her granddaughter Jane lived just a few blocks away.

Five people. Four cities. Four time zones. One grandmother they all loved.

In the past, this meant group texts, missed calls, and the constant feeling that someone, somewhere, was out of the loop. But when the family set up an Echo Show 8 in Mary's kitchen and connected everyone through the Alexa app, everything changed. It wasn't just a device anymore — it became the center of their Caregiver's Tree.

**The Shared Calendar**

The first thing they set up was a shared calendar.

Elena added all of Mary's medical appointments.

Daniel added reminders for medication refills.

Jane added her weekly visit schedule.

Carl added a repeating reminder: "Call Grandma every Sunday."

Mary didn't have to open an app or read a screen.

She simply asked, "Alexa, what's on my schedule today?"

And Alexa+ read it to her, clearly and calmly.

For the first time, the whole family saw the same information at the same time. No confusion. No crossed wires. No guilt about forgetting something important.

**Daily Check-Ins**

Every morning at 9 a.m., Alexa+ gently reminded Mary to take her blood pressure medication. At 10 a.m., she got a reminder to stretch and walk around the house. At noon, Alexa+ announced, "Time to drink water," a routine her doctor had recommended.

These weren't nagging reminders — they were small acts of care, delivered by a voice she trusted.

And if Mary ever needed someone, she didn't have to search for a phone.

- "Alexa, call Elena."

- "Alexa, message Daniel."
- "Alexa, drop in on Jane."

Communication became effortless.

It gave the family peace of mind — and it gave Mary confidence. She didn't feel monitored. She felt supported.

**The Moment Everything Made Sense**

One afternoon, Mary slipped while reaching for a mixing bowl. She wasn't hurt, but she was startled. She sat down at the kitchen table and said, "Alexa, call Jane."

Within seconds, Jane answered through the Echo Show.

"Are you okay, Grandma?"

"I'm fine," Mary said, "I just needed to hear your voice."

Jane came over anyway, but the important part was this:

Mary didn't panic.

She didn't feel alone.

She didn't have to wait for someone to check in.

The Caregiver's Tree worked exactly as it was meant to.

### A Family Reconnected

What surprised the family most wasn't the technology — it was the closeness it created.

Carl, thousands of miles away, could drop in and talk to his grandmother as if he were sitting in her kitchen.

Daniel could update her calendar from Miami.

Elena could check in during her lunch break.

Jane could stop by when needed.

And Mary?

She felt more connected than she had in years.

Alexa+ didn't replace the family. It united them. It gave each branch of the Caregiver's Tree a way to support the root — the person they all loved — without overwhelming any one person. It turned caregiving from a burden into a shared act of love.

# Final Chapter

I wrote this book to keep things simple and to shine a light on Ambient AI, Alexa+, and the Caregiver's Tree. Today, nearly one in four adults in the United States is providing ongoing care to a loved one, and that number continues to grow.

My hope is that the ideas in this book show how Alexa+ can transform caregiving from a heavy burden into a shared act of love — something families do together, with confidence, clarity, and connection. If this book helps even a fraction of those millions of caregivers feel more supported, then it has done its job.

If you know someone with low vision, including conditions like macular degeneration, I can help them as well. I have spent 35 years working with individuals who are blind or visually impaired, and in July 2025 I wrote *Navigating Life with Low Vision*, a book that explains the technology and local services available to support independence.

In that book, I highlight how Alexa has become an invaluable tool for individuals who are blind, low vision, or visually impaired — offering hands-free, voice-controlled access to information, communication, and daily tasks. I also cover every major category of assistive technology and provide local resources for every state. What makes *Navigating Life with Low Vision* so valuable is that it includes more than 100 pages of state-by-state resources so Veterans and individuals with low vision can quickly find the help they need.

When it comes to Alexa Plus, my goal is to continue building the KISS Alexa website and the YouTube channel @kissalexa. These spaces are designed for learning, sharing, and supporting one another. Tell your stories, ask your questions, and help others discover what's possible when technology becomes a bridge instead of a barrier.

Caregiving is one of the most human things we do. It asks us to show up, to stay connected, and to love in practical ways. My hope is that Alexa+ gives you tools that make that journey easier — not by replacing the human touch, but by strengthening it.

May your family find comfort, independence, and joy in the small moments you create together.

I wish you and your family success in everything you do.

Truly yours,

**Patrick J. Fischer**

# Appendix A - Understanding the Cost of Alexa+

You can get Alexa+ for $19.99 a month, or if you have Amazon Prime it comes included for free. Amazon Prime is a membership available for $14.99/month or pay $139.00 for a year and it is only $11.58 a month.

The math is pretty clear - if you want Alexa+, Prime is the better deal since you're getting way more bang for your buck at a lower price point.

With Amazon Prime you get a lot of great services including Alexa+, you also get fast reliable shipping along with access to Alexa+, and entertainment like Prime Video, Prime Music, and exclusive deals. It's designed to bundle convenience, savings, and digital perks into one simple subscription.

**Amazon Prime Pricing**

Monthly Option:

- $14.99/month - Monthly Prime membership

Annual Option:

- $139/year - Annual Prime membership (works out to about $11.58/month)

**Amazon Prime Benefits**

Shipping & Delivery:

- FREE Two-Day Delivery on millions of items
- FREE One-Day Delivery on 15+ million items

- FREE Same-Day Delivery on 3+ million items in eligible areas
- Ultrafast Grocery Delivery - Same-day grocery delivery
- Amazon Key - In-garage delivery option
- Release-Date Delivery - Get new releases on launch day

**Streaming & Entertainment:**

- Prime Video - Movies, series, documentaries, live sports with X-Ray features
- Amazon Music - 100+ million songs in shuffle mode, ad-free podcasts
- Prime Reading - Access to free books and magazines
- Prime Gaming - Free games and in-game content

**Shopping Perks:**

- Exclusive Deals - Prime Day and member-only discounts
- Early Access - Get first dibs on Lightning Deals
- Whole Foods Discounts - Special pricing for Prime members
- Try Before You Buy - Clothing program to test items first

**Additional Services:**

- FREE Grubhub+ - Unlimited $0 delivery fees on food orders
- Fuel Savings - $0.10 per gallon at bp, Amoco, and other stations
- Amazon Photos - Unlimited photo storage + 5GB video storage
- Prescription Discounts - Savings on medications

Alexa+ & Amazon Prime Pricing Breakdown

Alexa+ Subscription Pricing

For Prime Members:

- FREE - Alexa+ is included at no additional cost with your Prime membership

For Non-Prime Customers:

- $19.99/month - Standalone Alexa+ subscription for unlimited access

Key Points

- Both Prime and standalone Alexa+ offer identical unlimited access across all devices (Echo, web, app)

**Bottom Line:** If you're already a Prime member, you get Alexa+ thrown in for free. If not, you're looking at either $14.99/month for Prime (which includes Alexa+ plus all the other Prime perks) or $19.99/month for just Alexa+.

www.ingramcontent.com/pod-product-compliance
Lightning Source LLC
LaVergne TN
LVHW010544100826
845148LV00013B/2593
* 9 7 9 8 2 1 8 6 8 8 7 7 6 *